A FAIRWAY TO WALK

A Fairway to Walk

INSPIRATION FOR YOUR ROUND OF LIFE

John McCall

JWM Publishing

A FAIRWAY TO WALK

Copyright © 2021 by John McCall

Cover © 2021 by John McCall

Primary Editor: Stacey Smekofske – www.editsbystacey.com

Cover and Interior Formatting: Stacey Smekofske

Published by JWM Publishing

All rights reserved. For use of any part of this publication, whether reproduced, transmitted in any form or by any means, electronic, mechanical, photocopying, recording, or otherwise, or stored in a retrieval system, without the prior consent of the publisher, is an infringement of copyright law and is forbidden. The information presented herein is in no way intended as a substitute for counseling and other forms of professional guidance.

ISBNs

Paperback: 978-1-7370968-0-1

Hardcover: 978-1-7370968-2-5

Digital: 978-1-7370968-1-8

First Printing

Dedication

My wife Marla...the most understanding, long-suffering, loving and caring individual I have ever met...
And
My children, Jennifer, Christopher and Shannon, who will always be my most precious authorship.

Acknowledgments

Many thanks to Michael Gee, who encouraged me from the very beginning, in the way only a treasured friend can.

Thanks to my editor, Stacey Smekofske, who used her expertise to encourage a first-time author who was more than willing to be led by the hand.

A very special thank you to my most wonderful wife, Marla, who has stood by my side at every turn in our lives together, cheering me on.

Contents

Introduction	xi
Faith	1
Faith is a Gift	5
Trust Your Beliefs	7
Truth is Close	11
Humility	13
A Single Step	15
Compassion	17
A Member of the Church	19
Righteousness	21
Good Order of a Man's Life	23
Grace	25
The Great Commission	27
Discipline	29
Fall Into His Hands	31
Serving With Gratitude	33
What If	35
Patience	37
The Glory of Life	39
Being Christian	41
Treasure God Above All	43
Repentance	45
Appreciation	47
Sycamore	49
Where Would We Be	53
Confidence	55
There Is One God	57
Warriors Of The Faith	59
A Psalm	63
Balance	65
We are Given All Things	67
Worthiness	69
Moment in Prayer	71

Contentment	73
Because of Jesus	75
Forgiveness	77
He Chose You	79
Dactylogram Of Christ	81
Peace	85
Liberty	87
Moral Leadership	89
The Tee, The Cross And Resurrection	91
He is no Fool	93
Traditions	95
A Prayer in Rebirth	97
About The Author	99

Introduction

My journey to a more mature faith is far from completed. I acknowledge this to the reader in order for you not to think your author has reached some pinnacle to which the reader cannot. Your pinnacle may be completely different from mine. I believe I haven't reached that point of complete maturity, nor perfectness in my walk with Christ. Life's journey is far too bumpy in nature, creating many questions in the form of pitfalls where one may believe they have reached maturity only to find out they have just barely begun the walk.

At the age of 43, I reached a point in my life in which I acknowledged the need for a more mature relationship of faith in Christ. I found I did not know how to begin, much less how to know when I had arrived at that precious point.

I am thankful that through association with believers, a very kind and understanding pastor of a small church in Central Idaho, and a very good friend who took the time to talk and pray with me, I was able to prepare myself for a moment I did not realize was coming so quickly. After five years of searching, I was led to the Lord by a 95-year-old retired pastor who was to later become my father-in-law.

If you are a Christian already given over to our Lord, stay the path.

Introduction

If you are searching, do not quit. If you are seeking a way out of the doldrums of your life, read on. The essays that follow are for you.

My hope is you will find unclaimed treasures for yourselves in each reading. May you be unrestricted in your searching; may you be open to our Master's leading in your life.

Be encouraged as you continue your journey to a more mature faith.

Faith

"And He said unto them, Where is your faith? And they being afraid wondered, saying one to another, What manner of man is this? For He commandeth even the winds and water, and they obey," (St. Luke 8:25, KJV).

What does it take to have faith like that of the Lord? What must one have within himself to have a faith so strong? Why are we not given this kind of unmovable faith from our birth? What is the road to a more mature faith?

Using the analogy of a round of golf, I will guide you down that fairway and identify a few yard markers. Just as in your last round at your favorite course, start at the beginning. The tee box is in this case where you find yourself at this moment. As in all your efforts, have an aim in mind, a goal, and in golf it is a green with a very small hole, which no doubt seems smaller the further you are from it.

You will need to take firm strokes, with good advice, and constant practice to manage a game that allows you to arrive at the hole with confidence. You will no doubt gain more faith and confidence in your swing and in your abilities as you practice and play more. Once you reach the green, just as in life, there seems to be no sure way to reach your goal. No lines on the surface of the green, no grooves to place the ball in to ensure it reaches the hole, no guaranteed formula to gauge speed and distance.

What gives us the self-confidence to draw on under any circumstance? It is Christ! Without Christ actively walking with us as we wind our way, we will find ourselves in the rough, in the bunkers, in the water, and some may even find themselves out of bounds. We cannot expect to have a faith that is as strong as Jesus', after all, He is God. What we can obtain is that He is not only the object of our faith, but He is the seed that has been in us from our birth. We need only to recognize that He is the embodiment of our faith. Once you have felt the tugging on your heart to turn to Him, He will move in ways that will bring you closer to Him.

Thus, it is a humbleness that we must find in our life's game that will bring us to our knees where we can find that faith which was instilled in us from our beginning. We should allow ourselves to set a new goal, survey the fairway and the greens of our lives, consider our abilities, take an all-important stance, and begin the faith walk of our lives through the course laid out before us.

The Bible says, "Faith cometh by hearing, and hearing by the word of God" (Romans 10:17, KJV).

It is hard to hear the word of God if you do not read the word of God. Just as it is hard to play the game of golf if you do not read the rules and learn how to play. We learn how to have faith by reading His word, trusting what He says, and doing His work.

I have never been to Augusta National, but I know it to be there. I have seen it on TV when watching the Masters Tournament and have read about it in books and magazines. I have faith in the folks who put it on TV, and I believe the folks who write the articles. Yes, I have faith they are telling the truth.

To quote Reverend Billy Graham, "Faith isn't pretending our problems don't exist, nor is it simply blind optimism. Faith points us beyond our problems to the hope we have in Christ," (Billy Graham in Quotes, pg. 135, 2011).

If we work on maturing what faith we have, we will rise above the doubting and come to a point of complete trust. We would solve a lot of our on-course headaches if we could completely trust our game. Faith is the victory!

Faith is a Gift

D.L. MOODY-SPEAKING OF THE REALITY OF FAITH.

"Faith is the gift of God. So is the air, but you have to breathe it.

So is bread, but you have to eat it.

So is water, but you have to drink it.

Some people are wanting a miraculous kind of feeling.

That is not faith: 'Faith cometh by hearing and hearing by the Word of God.' (Romans 10:17 KJV)

It is not for me to sit down and wait for faith to come stealing over me with some strange sensation, but to take God at His Word. You cannot believe unless you have something to believe. So take the Bible as it is written, and appropriate it."

Trust Your Beliefs

"For thou art my hope, O Lord God: Thou art my trust from my youth," (Psalm 71:5, KJV).

From a very young age we are taught to trust what our mothers, fathers, schoolteachers, pastors, scoutmasters, and many other authority figures tell us. They encourage us to *believe* what they say and teach us. When we are young, we tend not to doubt, but to take what we have been told or taught as the truth, trusting we have been given truthful information from the beginning.

What happens to that trust? As we get older, we may doubt what we have been told to believe is the truth. Just because truth may not be what you want to hear or believe doesn't change it from being the truth.

Truth is truth...timeless...never changing. If it is truth from its origin, then it remains the truth–even as it passes into history. History cannot be changed. We may not like parts of our history, but we cannot change what has already taken place or been spoken. Historical accounts of an event may be rewritten, but that does not change the actual event, it only changes what someone has said about the event. The actual happenings have not, nor will they ever change.

The gospel as proclaimed by our Lord Jesus Christ is indeed the good news. It was given centuries ago, and it remains the truth. Even though there may be many new translations of the Bible and our Savior's words, it does not change what He originally spoke. His original words remain in history just as He spoke them. They were written as they were received as the inspired word from God through the Holy Spirit to the individual writers. Again, you cannot change what He originally said, you can only change the words He spoke so that the following generations can better understand them. Thus, we have newer and different translations of the Bible.

Placing your trust in the word of God amounts to locking it up in your heart so that it can never be changed, and it never lessens in its impact. It is never watered down or diluted in such a fashion as to cause a person not to see the meaning or not to trust His word. You cannot change the past. Once words pass the lips, the good they do or the harm they inflict is unalterably beyond retraction.

Do you know what you believe? Do you believe what you know? We may believe what we have been taught to believe. We may believe what we have been told is the truth. When talking to His disciples the Lord said, "And ye shall know the truth, and the truth shall make you free," (John 8:32, KJV). As we have grown older, we have found that what we believe is up to each individual. You can trust what you have been taught, or you can choose to go in a completely different direction and believe whatever you might choose. But remember, your choice does not change history, it can only change how you see history.

As adults, we think for ourselves; we are able to decide about a subject or a theory, or even our faith. How can we go about that? How can we trust what we discover? What is the evidence supporting the truth?

Ah! ...the evidence. What is the evidence of our belief in God? His word? On what do we base our trust in what He says? Do we base it on results, answered prayers, changed lives, following repentance and acceptance? Is the world around us enough of a miracle to offer stand-alone proof? Is man's existence proof enough? Do miracles of healings fit in the proof somewhere? Does the miracle of the human body stand as the final proof alone?

The evidence is in His word; trusting His word as it speaks to our own heart. Believing what we have been taught is one thing. Reading His word for ourselves and trusting Him completely will seal His spoken word in our hearts. He is as close as your unspoken prayer. You only need to allow your heart to trust. You will find you know what you believe and will believe what you know, trusting Him as never before.

Truth is Close

JWM

Truth is as close to you as your Bible,
the Word of God.
Trusting the truth;
standing for the truth,
is a testament
to the strength of your belief.

Humility

"Humble yourselves therefore under the mighty hand of God, that He may exalt you in due time," (1 Peter 5:6, KJV).

Quite early in my golfing life, I realized it was a very humbling game.

To say that we all have not been humbled by the poor shot, the off-balance swing, poor putt, and the many missed opportunities would be a very bold misstatement. I haven't played for a long time. I wasn't afraid to be humbled in front of my playing partners, but my inability to play golf recently came from my back and shoulders giving out before my game did. Selling all my golf equipment was a very humbling experience. Now, I only watch and listen to golf, but I have not lost interest. What a game.

The road to a more mature faith is riddled with humbling moments, what-ifs, and a litany of oh-if-onlys. When Jesus initially reached out to His disciples and said, "Follow me," you can only imagine how that humbled each of them. "Who, me? You mean me?" Were they ready to follow? How would that change their lives? Were they even considering whether or not they were qualified? We have to step back a bit and remember where we were when we started playing golf. We were novices no doubt, amateurs for sure. We wanted what others had... a good game.

Some still want what others have, especially in a relationship with our Lord, Jesus Christ. It starts with acknowledging where you are now, accepting that you need to change. Drawing yourself down to the point where you can be honest with Him and yourself and accept the fact that we are sinners–all of us. When you humble yourself before God, He asks you to walk with Him. "He hath shown thee, O man, what is good; and what doth the Lord require of thee, but to do justly, and to love mercy, and to walk humbly with thy God," (Micah 6:8 KJV).

I no longer stand on the tee on a Wednesday morning and allow the breeze to refresh my eagerness to send the ball down the fairway. Oh, how I miss that feeling of driving the ball off the first tee and starting a new round. What a rush.

If you are reading this and are about to walk your favorite course, take a moment and realize the opportunity you have to start a new life, a life in Christ. There is nothing He cannot forgive, nothing that He cannot cover with His grace and mercy. Humble yourself before an all-forgiving God and your walk will be one with rewards that cannot be spoken.

It is up to each one of us to open the door of our heart to Him: "Behold I stand at the door, and knock: if any man hear my voice, and open the door, I will come in to him, and will sup with him, and he with me," (Revelation 3:20, KJV).

When we commit to follow Jesus Christ, we must put all else aside; step away from our pride and humble ourselves to serve Him. "God resisteth the proud, but giveth grace to the humble," (James 4:6 KJV). We commit to many things in our daily life, and particularly when we are on the course. We take a stand, we commit to our swing, and we follow through. If you apply that simple rule to a larger life scale, you will find that following Jesus places you on a path of righteousness–a road to a more mature faith.

A Single Step
THOMAS A. KEMPIS

"For a small reward, a man will hurry away on a long journey; while for eternal life, many will hardly take a single step."

Compassion

*J*esus called his disciples to him and said, "I have compassion for these people; they have already been with me three days and have nothing to eat. I do not want to send them away hungry, or they may collapse on the way," (Matthew 15:32, NIV).

This one act of compassion illustrates the definition: having a sympathetic consciousness of others' distress together with a desire to alleviate it. How else can one describe compassion? It is a term defined by the action taken by an individual or group who feels the need to help others.

Unlike empathy, which is the ability to relate to another person's pain vicariously, as if one has experienced that pain themselves. Compassion does not have to have the experience of having gone through an event yourself. You only have to understand the pain that one may be experiencing. Although Christ had served the 40 days without sustenance while being tempted by the devil, He did not have to go through an experience to know the peoples' pain. He is their Father, and like an earthly father our Heavenly Father knows each of His children's pain.

Jesus asked only what resources were available so that He might make a way for the thousands to be fed. Seven loaves and a few small fishes was the response. We all know the outcome of that meal...more was left over than had been provided at the outset. Compassion had been needed, provided for and spilled over, lest many would have gone hungry in their bellies and in their souls.

Galatians 6:2 NIV states, "Carry each other's burdens, and in this way, you will fulfill the law of Christ." The quote does not say that it removes the burdens entirely. It indicates the burdens are now shared and shouldered by another, removing the weight from the sufferer to the individual who has come along side to help carry the load. Nor does the quote indicate the burden is to be continuously shared over a great length of time. A time of restoration is called for when events bring someone to their knees. The compassionate serve for the needed period and then return to providing for their own needs, rebuilding strength to serve again.

"We then that are strong ought to bear the infirmities of the weak, and not to please ourselves," (Romans 15:1, NIV). In this quote, we might assume the word ought to be equated to the term indebtedness, requiring the strong to show compassion to the weak through mercy, sympathy, tenderness, and humaneness. Yes, even sorrow or pity can be shown when the distress or misfortune of another has come to our attention.

St. Luke 14: 1-14 is a great example of the full measure of compassion. I would challenge the reader to go to this passage. Read the words, recognizing the intent of Christ. Is it too much to ask that we realize the Father sent His Son to set the example for his children?

The ultimate compassion was the Father's gift of Christ on the cross. He gave his only Son to be the propitiation for sin–for you and me. He has the consciousness of our situation, the desire to alleviate the pain that situation has brought on, and the ability to bring each of us through the storm of heartache and anguish.

Accepting or giving, compassion will warm your heart!

A Member of the Church

AUTHOR UNKNOWN

A member of the church, who previously had been attending services regularly, stopped going. After a few weeks, the pastor decided to visit him.

It was a chilly evening. The pastor found the man at home alone, sitting before a blazing fire. Guessing the reason for his pastor's visit, the man welcomed him, led him to a comfortable chair near the fireplace and waited.

The pastor made himself at home but said nothing. In the grave silence, he contemplated the dance of the flames around the burning logs. After some minutes, the pastor took the fire tongs, carefully picked up a brightly burning ember and placed it to one side of the hearth all alone then he sat back in his chair, still silent.

The host watched all this in quiet contemplation. As the one lone ember's flame flickered and diminished, there was a momentary glow and then its fire was no more. Soon it was cold and dead.

Not a word had been spoken since the initial greeting. The pastor glanced at his watch and realized it was time to leave. He slowly stood up, picked up the cold, dead ember and placed it back in the middle of the fire. Immediately it began to glow, once more with the light and warmth of the burning coals around it.

As the pastor reached the door to leave, his host said with a tear running down his cheek, 'Thank you so much for your visit and especially for the fiery sermon. I will be back in church next Sunday.'

We live in a world today, which tries to say too much with too little. Consequently, few listen. Sometimes the best sermons are the ones left unspoken.

Righteousness

"Blessed are they which do hunger and thirst after righteousness: for they shall be filled," (Matthew 5:6, KJV.)

"The hardest shot is a mashie at ninety yards from the green, where the ball has to be played against an oak tree, bounced back into a sand trap, hits a stone, bounces onto the green, and then rolls into the cup. That shot is so difficult I have only made it once," (Zeppo Marx).

What exactly is righteousness? It certainly is not being right all the time; nor is it being the wisest of the wise. However, it is doing according to that which is right. I have failed at that many times. Every day I find something in myself that I can identify as not being righteous. Is a small fib the same as a lie? Do I tell my opponent I moved my ball with my foot to get a better lie? Do I claim the once in a lifetime shot as Zeppo Marx did? Maybe he actually made that shot ... but...was he really trying to do it that way?

When we place our feet on the path to a mature faith, we must ask ourselves if we have what it takes to go the distance. Acknowledging that we cannot do it with only our own strength is the first in many steps down that fairway. After all, the fairway was clear when we stood on the tee, but somehow, we seem to interrupt the tranquility of the walk with our first step onto the grass. We disturb the walk with our own banter, chipping up pieces of sod with each swing, then show our exasperation with a missed chip or putt. First, we have to admit we are not perfect. Flawed is an oft-used term, but we can improve or be made over.

We do have an advocate, the Holy Spirit, who will help us in our walk–our life's caddie, so to speak. Helping us walk the fairways of our lives with constant encouragement to walk upright, remain prudent in our actions, and wise in our decisions. We must listen to Him.

In our foursome, we may hear many voices, some more pleasing than others. What we must do is listen to that small inner voice which guides us on our walk. That voice will filter the conversations, help you in your conscious decisions, and will certainly not lead you into the rough along life's fairway.

"Wherefore seeing we also are compassed about with so great a cloud of witnesses, let us lay aside every weight, and the sin which doth so easily beset us, and let us run with patience the race that is set before us," (Hebrews 12:1, KJV).

Living an upright life is not easy, just look at what the disciples endured and what Christ himself endured. Each step we take should be one emboldened by the word of God; the strength of His word should give you the feeling of His armor shielding your life from the stones and arrows of sin and ridicule. You are your Father's creation, and He did not create man to fail. Your walk can be one of strength and uprightness. Your game can be a winner regardless of the score penciled on your card. Being confident in your uprightness, your inner wisdom and your righteousness will bring you rewards you never imagined.

You cannot learn the game of golf merely by reading Harvey Penick's Little Red Book, you have to get out on the course and swing the clubs. You cannot walk the fairways of life with righteousness in your heart unless you read and live by God's word.

"All scripture is given by inspiration of God, and is profitable for doctrine, for reproof, for correction, for instruction in righteousness," (2 Timothy 3:16, KJV).

Good Order of a Man's Life

JWM

The good order of a man's life,
reflects the true measure of his character.

Grace

"For by grace are ye saved through faith; and that not of yourselves: it is the gift of God: not of works, lest any man should boast," (Ephesians 2:8-9, KJV).

This is a passage with which we are all very familiar, yet do we truly understand the meaning and the price paid in order for each of us to receive such a gift? There has never been, nor will there ever be, a greater agony than that which was dealt to Christ on the cross. Yet as He hung there, He forgave the executioners, and those who had called for his death, for the unimaginable agony He was enduring. Still, He stretches out his grace-filled hand to us.

This grace is given such that, "In the ages to come He might show the exceeding riches of His grace in His kindness toward us through Christ Jesus." (Eph. 2:7, KJV). We can all recall the well-known quote, "Grace is getting something we don't deserve while mercy is not getting what we do deserve," (Anon). Grace and mercy are like unto the two sides of the same coin. Still, we struggle with grasping the unfathomable gift that is given us. It is not for His promise of riches that we accept his gift. It is because we are sinners, and He is providing the path for our forgiveness and renewal, accepting what his promise offers. Only then He rewards us even more. That there would be riches beyond our being forgiven, escapes our mind. We need not wonder at what those riches might be; be assured they are far beyond our own imagining.

"Amazing Grace, how sweet the sound, that saved a wretch like me!

I once was lost, but now am found-was blind, but now I see," (John Newton).

It is hard for most people to put behind them a past that includes the sins committed, both big and small (as we see them). We have trouble forgiving ourselves of those indiscretions and setting them aside on some shelf to be forgotten. We may never be able to forget them, but understanding that His grace covers all those *unforgettables,* allows us to stand tall and to continue our lives with the assurance that through Christ the Father sees us as spotless. As hard to understand as that may seem, we need only to kneel and thank God for the atoning sacrifice that Christ paid on the cross. Repent. Accept His gift and move forward with a new capacity to accomplish his purpose.

"The motive of grace is the infinite, compassionate love of a merciful God, but the work of grace was the death of Christ on the cross," (Rev. Billy Graham).

A heartfelt...Amen!

The Great Commission
PASTOR KEITH WILSON

"Jesus' authoritative call on the lives of all His followers to teach people of every tribe and tongue to worship at the feet of an all-sufficient, ever present Savior."

Hood Canal Community Church, 7-14-19

Discipline

"Commit to the Lord whatever you do, and your plans will succeed," (Proverbs 16:3, NIV).

What does one have to do to commit to the Lord? Is there something special one has to do to garner His favor? Are there some extra meaningful words one has to repeat or a special prayer one has to pray? Just what does it take to commit with discipline?

"It took me seventeen years to get three thousand hits in baseball. I did it in one afternoon on the golf course," (Hank Aaron).

Discipline is the basis of a true commitment. I remember the day I was chasing my children around in our backyard. I was a young father in the Air Force, enjoying my children at play. Then with almost no breath, I came to a total stop, gasping for air; I had finally reached the point which had been coming for several years. I was a smoker and I had to stop. I had tried many times before, but this was it, the final straw. It would only get worse. The next morning, I rid myself of all my ghastly smoking paraphernalia and went to work determined to discipline myself to never smoke again. That was over forty years ago. Disciplined by my own words and a commitment to be successful.

If Hank Aaron had not had the discipline as a young man to keep swinging at balls pitched to him as a youth, do you really think he would have become a home-run king? Do you think you can become a better golfer if you hit more balls, play more rounds, keep changing the clubs you use? With discipline you can most assuredly improve your game.

Your walk with our Lord takes a might more than just talking about it; it takes commitment, discipline to read His Word, and effort to serve Him. My earthly father called hard work "preparation." Be prepared. You cannot be properly prepared to tackle a 568-yard, par 5, with water down the left side and three traps on the right, if you are not disciplined to practice with a commitment to succeed. Our Lord calls on us to commit whatever we do to Him and we will succeed.

In his book, *Disciplines of a Godly Man*, Senior Pastor R. Kent Hughes states, "...discipline is God-centered. The legalistic heart says, I will do this thing to gain merit with God. The disciplined heart says, I will do this thing because I love God and want to please Him," (Disciplines of a Godly Man, pg. 15, 10th Anniversary Addition). Place in your heart the firm commitment to do your best for Him. He gave all for you, so that you can have a full life on this earth with preparations for a life eternally with Him.

Our golf game spoils when we do not practice or play the courses. Likewise, our relationship to our Heavenly Father grows cold when we do not read His word, speak to Him in prayer and follow His outline for our lives.

I always wanted to break par when I was playing. Truthfully, I never broke 80. Par was a dream, a goal, but like you I am sure, I kept trying. Your prayer today could be one of asking the Lord to help you attain a particular goal which you could not reach. You might also ask Him to strengthen your discipline and give you a commitment that is bolstered by His own hand. Breaking par may not be your goal, maybe it is breaking 80. Commit to a discipline of practice, both on the course and in your renewed walk with your Lord.

No, there are no special words to say, nothing special you have to do, other than offering up a prayer asking your Father in Heaven to give you renewed strength in your discipline with a commitment to succeed.

Fall Into His Hands

HEBREWS 10:31 KJV

"It is a fearful thing to fall into the hands of the living God."

Serving With Gratitude

"Serve wholeheartedly, as if you were serving the Lord, not men, because you know that the Lord will reward everyone for whatever good he does, whether he is slave or free," (Ephesians 6:7-8, NIV).

Serving with a thankful heart is a cornerstone of the Christian way of living. It is what Jesus has asked us to do, to serve others rather than ourselves. It is what He did while experiencing his time here on earth.

Just what does that service call us to do, or better yet what can we bring to the table to show our thankfulness for the opportunity to serve? If we do as He has asked us to do, "Not with eyeservice, as men pleasers; but as the servants of Christ, doing the will of God from the heart," (Ephesians 6:6 KJV) should we do it with a feeling of personal responsibility or should we do it with a feeling of obligation? The answer is we do it because we have an obligation to unite privilege with responsibility.

We, especially in this country, have a strong historical basis for showing our gratitude for all the privileges we have been given as citizens. If you have ever had the opportunity to work and/or live outside the United States, you will have no doubt felt that responsibility. We have extraordinary opportunities as citizens, and as fellow human beings, to not only help our neighbors but to pay back to our country some of what has been given by past generations.

Past generations did not have the sophistication that is available today, yet they built a nation that has stood on the same constitution for over 225 years. Our founding fathers declared us an independent nation in 1776 and stood by it. They established our nation as a republic in 1789 and have stood by it through many wars and conflicts. Do we owe these previous generations their due? By all accounts...yes!

The apostles were not qualified when Jesus called them to follow him. He qualified them as they listened to him, as they watched him, as they saw his interaction with those he loved, which was everyone. He instilled in them the capacity if you will, to do good to accomplish his purpose. Most humbly, Christ emptied himself to those who would open the door to their hearts and ask him in. He did it then, and he does it still today! He will qualify each of us as we answer his call to be a servant. Growth in the ministry of serving is not counted in the larger numbers of those who yield themselves to serving, but in the growth, in and of the heart, of those who do serve. Just think - what can be accomplished if you apply your God-given talents to the task?

What can we do? Open our hearts to his leadership in our lives. Accept that it is He who can empower each of us to serve unselfishly. What can we bring to the table? We can bring a willingness to serve, a loving and giving heart, our first fruits. We need only to hear Him, obey Him and act as He has asked us to...to serve.

Showing our gratitude to those who have gone before us is a responsibility of each citizen. Likewise, showing our gratitude, thankfulness and love to our Heavenly Father is an obligation that each of us should feel stronger than any other emotion. Indeed, uniting privilege with responsibility is our obligation to our fellow man; those who we can reach now, and those who have gone on before us who are responsible for us arriving at our time with the privileges we so enjoy.

"May our gratitude find expression in our prayers and our service for others, and in our commitment to live wholly for Christ," (Rev. Billy Graham).

What If

AUTHOR UNKNOWN

What if you woke up this morning,
 With only what you thanked God for yesterday?

Patience

"But they that wait upon the Lord shall renew their strength; they shall mount up with wings as eagles; they shall run, and not be weary; and they shall walk, and not faint," (Isaiah 40:31, KJV).

God is greater than our circumstances! His power is supreme. His creation is grander than our finite minds can even imagine; yet He knows the moment a small bird falls to the ground. His patience with His creation is beyond our understanding. We are called to wait on Him. "Wait on the Lord: be of good courage, and He shall strengthen thine heart: wait, I say, on the Lord," (Psalm 27:14, KJV).

Henry Longhurst was a British golf writer and commentator. He was a golf correspondent for the Sunday Times for 45 years and a member of the British Parliament during World War II. He was inducted into the World Golf Hall of Fame in September 2017. He once said, "If you call on God to improve the results of a shot while it is still in motion, you are using 'an outside agency' and subject to appropriate penalties under the rules of golf."

I do not think God is going to respond to such a request in any circumstance. That instant, after you hit the ball, that agonizing instant when you know your shot was not hit squarely, your body twists, your tongue goes to one side of your cheek, words tumble out of your mouth in exasperation, and you call for divine intervention! You realize you will have to wait to see just what kind of a lie you will have. Your patience is tested; you would like a mulligan, but it is not allowed. You are in a hurry, but the yardage is approaching 240. "Patience," your caddie says. You need to use the time to gather yourself up for the next shot.

Do you do that with the other areas of your life? Are you impatient? Do you want to hurry through your day, get out of the office or off the ladder, or out of traffic? Regardless of where we find ourselves, we need to learn to react with calmness. We should be expectant but without being discontent. Being patient denotes a calm endurance.

Our lives should be an example of character. Patience relates to being strong in times of trouble, times of provocation, times of ill treatment, or times when we feel like retaliating. Comments from your playing partners can sometimes ruin your round, not just your scoring, but your time together. In fact, your entire day can be askew following just one thoughtless comment. Guard yourself from quick responses that may provoke to your fellow players. "Let your moderation be known unto all men. The Lord is at hand," (Philippians 4:5, KJV). There are times when patience is indeed a virtue, more so than others. You want to be a good witness for the faith. Some say many times that the only Bible someone may come in contact with is you. What word are you spreading? What character are you showing to others?

I admit that patience is one tough attribute to get a handle on. You cannot master it by yourself. It takes working at it 24/7. The road to a mature faith is a long continuing journey and will take character, stamina, and patience. When you step out to follow Christ, you take a step along a road that is unlike any other. The fruit of your walk will be a testament to your patience. When Christ was relating the parable of the seeds He stated, "But that on the good ground are they, which in an honest and good heart, having heard the Word, keep it, and bring forth fruit with patience," (Luke 8:15, KJV).

The Glory of Life

JWM

The glory of life is to love,
Not to be loved;
To give,
Not to get;
To serve, not to be served.

Being Christian

"For by grace are ye saved through faith; and that not of yourselves: it is the gift of God: Not of works, lest any man should boast," (Ephesians 2:8-9, KJV).

On what basis are you going to stand before a perfect holy God and say that you have been good enough? Are we really worthy of the gift He offers each of us?

We are all already under God's judgement, because everyone has violated his moral law. God sees everyone the same; yes, some are worse than others, but we trust He will judge them rightly because He is the perfect holy judge. Would we expect that the creator of the universe would be anything else but the perfect judge? After all, He is the only one capable of perfect justice. Left for man to be the judge, as flawed as he is, justice could never be levied with anything close to perfection. Be it for the Mother Teresas of the world or the diabolical Osama Bin Ladens of recent history, or for even the author of this work, justice is fair in the hands of a holy God.

Intake: Becoming a Christian means you repent of your sins and accept Him as your Lord and Savior and turn your life over to Him. You accept all that He is, and all He asks you to do.

"He is no fool who gives up what he cannot keep, to gain what he cannot lose," (Christian Martyr Jim Elliott).

Outpouring: Being Christian means living a life in which you share the fruits of the spirit at every opportunity, take a stand for Jesus and accept His grace, mercy, forgiveness, and justice, and choose to live by His Holy Word. "Verily I say unto you, inasmuch as ye have done it unto one of the least of these my brethren, ye have done it unto me," (Matthew 25:40, KJV).

Recognizing what is offered, accepting what is given as a gift, and realizing what eternal benefits are derived, would be a great loss to those who turn their back on the one true God? Many religions claim to have the only true god, yet no other religion, or belief system, can point back to the biblical and secular historians who documented Jesus' life through thousands of both biblical and secular manuscripts that record the history of Jesus Christ. These documents prove who Jesus was and what He did.

Many believed that the world was flat until proven wrong. Many believed man could not ever leave the surly bonds of earth, but he has. What some people believe, will work for them for a while, but the truth always seems to work its way to the surface. Then beliefs change, expectations change based on new information. Yet the case for a living god continues to be reinforced. No other religion claims a living god. Why would they? If they accept the concept of a living god, they would then be subject to that god. The Christian believes in the one true living God, as the Father, the Son and the Holy Ghost.

"The fear of the Lord is the beginning of knowledge, but fools despise wisdom and instruction," (Proverbs 1:7, KJV).

Being open to God's leadership in your life is the most refreshing thing you can do, outside of salvation itself. Becoming a Christian is the beginning...being Christian is the life you lead.

"We aren't only called to become Christian; we are also called to be Christian," (Rev. Billy Graham).

God's justice will be perfect and final. Choose to live for Him!

Treasure God Above All

PASTOR KEITH WILSON

"Sin is preferring anything more than I prefer God.
It is a failure of the heart to not treasure God above all else."

Hood Canal Community Church, 2-9-20

Repentance

"For thus the Lord God, the Holy One of Israel, has said, 'In repentance and rest you shall be saved, in quietness and trust is your strength.' But you were not willing," (Isaiah 30:15, NASB).

If you are not familiar with the above quote, don't be surprised, not many are. Our unfamiliarity sometimes gives us the excuse to not do as we are told. Webster's Dictionary (5th Ed.) defines repent as, "To amend or resolve to amend one's life as a result of contrition for one's sins. To change one's mind with regard to past or intended action, conduct, etc., on account of regret or dissatisfaction." Regret? Dissatisfaction? Oh yes, we all have regrets and dissatisfactions in our lives, but what do we do about them?

Jesus said "Repent, for the kingdom of heaven is at hand," (Matthew 4:17 NASB). You cannot build a larger golf course in the place of the old; you only have the land you have, and you must work within the limits it gives you. After years of use and abuse from players, equipment and weather, there comes a time when changes have to be made. Reconstruction is the answer, and a total transformation is the goal. So, it is with our lives, recognizing and admitting that we need to repent of our sins. We get a whole new start to our life through Christ. Reconstruction and transformation are made through the strength provided by

God. Turning from sin is our part in His plan. God accomplishes the conversion through his forgiving.

Sometimes we think that repentance only applies to the big sins in our lives, not the small, insignificant little items that we tend to allow to go unnoticed. This is not so. Remember the little kick you gave the ball some time ago to get it back into a playable position. Remember the sharp tone of voice you used when replying to a fellow players retort. Taken to heart, repentance is the one thing that will allow us to start that reclamation of the course of our lives, bringing into our lives the fresh air, sunshine and freedom that living a life in Christ affords you. Living a repentant life in Christ is not restrictive as many think. It is the ultimate freedom. You must be willing to change.

Don't let the process get in the way of the rewards that will be forthcoming. If you have had a swing coach, or just a session or two with the local pro, you will remember that he works with what you have or what you bring to the game. Then he begins to reshape your stance, your posture at address or your timing. How many times did he say, "Don't worry about the distance, that will come, let's get the basics first"? So, let us concentrate on the basics in our walk with our Lord. Let us do what needs to be done first. Repent, turn from our wicked ways and begin to savor the life we were put here to enjoy.

Appreciation

JWM

We should live in appreciation
For what Christ has done for each of us.

Without that appreciation for Him,
We idolize ourselves,
And
Indulge our wickedness.

Sycamore

Webster's Collegiate Dictionary 1947 Fifth Edition defines the word Sycamore as, "A tree of Egypt and Asia Minor, often called sycamore fig, useful as a shade tree and having fruit that is sweet and edible. This is the sycamore of Scripture." It goes on until at the end of its definition it states that it is "a plane tree." Webster further defines "plane" as in "plane tree" to be "on account of its broad leaves and spreading form."

"And JESUS entered and passed through Jericho. And behold, there was a man Zacchaeus, which was a chief among the publicans, and he was rich, And he sought to see Jesus who he was; and could not for the press, because he was of little stature. And he ran before and climbed up into a sycamore tree to see him: for he was to pass that way. And when Jesus came to the place, he looked up, and saw him, and said unto him, Zacchaeus, make haste, and come down; for today I must abide in thy house. And he made haste, and came down, and received him joyfully," (St. Luke 19: 1-6, KJV).

How often have we stood behind the crowd, straining our necks to see what pageantry might be passing us by without our knowing? As a child it was commonplace to hold my father's hand at a parade and tug and tug until he raised me up so that I could clearly see what was so strikingly interesting to the crowds which had assembled. Remember being in your parents' safe grasp as they carried you along on even simple daily journeys? We all have such memories, yet we seem to lose them over the months and years of our growing up. What would we have missed had our parents not raised us up? What might we have done had we not had that experience? We were lifted to see better, and our field of vision would be uncluttered by all that was going on around us. We were raised so that our experience would be full.

It was the same with Zacchaeus. We don't know a lot about him except that in St. Luke 19:9 KJV Jesus calls him, "A son of Abraham." After all, he was a Jew and as a tax collector, he was not loved by his fellow citizens and was considered a sinner. However, he was drawn to Christ. Acknowledging Zacchaeus up in the tree, Jesus drew attention to a less than desirable member of his community; possibly, he was one who had taken advantage of his fellow Jews. He was a sinner who Jesus had come to save.

Zacchaeus hosted Jesus in his home that evening. During that time of breaking bread, he would come to truly know his Savior as Jesus spoke the words, "This day is salvation come to this house, forsomuch as he is also a son of Abraham. For the Son of man is come to seek and save that which was lost" (St. Luke 19:9-10, KJV).

Zacchaeus did not climb the tree to be saved, but to get a better view and to be closer to Jesus. He climbed the tree to have the experience of the moment. Maybe exposure is all that is needed, the experience of coming closer to our Savior. If you are feeling that desire to learn more about our Savior, then rise up, reach out, and accept the change in your life as your heart is filled with the Holy Spirit.

What do we need to raise us up to see Jesus? Probably not a sycamore tree, probably not even a tree at all. What might cloud our vision so that we cannot see our heavenly Father standing just before us calling us to him.? Could it be the drudge of everyday chores? Our financial situation? Our marriage or relationship going wrong? Maybe it's a boss who seems not to understand your workload or a teacher who ignores your efforts despite your challenges.

Maybe we do not need to rise at all. Our sycamore may be the floor in our bedroom as we rest in prayer against our bedside. It may be the pause at the water fountain at work to cool off that roiling anger at someone's poorly chosen words after viewing your proposal. It may be the moment you have at your school locker; it could be those few seconds when you can say to yourself, "I know Him! I know He sees me where I am! I do not have to be in view of Him, as He is always in view of me! Raise me up, Father. Give me full view of my life from your prospective, not mine. Refresh my spirit. Raise me up that I may see you clearly. Show me my sycamore tree."

Where Would We Be

AUTHOR UNKNOWN

Where would we be without Jesus?
He was born of a woman...
So He could be born of God.
He humbled Himself...
So we could be lifted up.
He became a servant...
So we could be made heirs.
He suffered rejection...
So we could become His friends.
He denied Himself...
So we could freely receive all things.
He gave Himself...
So He could bless us every way.

Confidence

"It is better to trust in the Lord than to put confidence in man," (Psalm 118:8, KJV).

Have you heard that quote before? Maybe you heard it as, "It is better to put your *trust* in the Lord than man." If you are on the course and you need your caddie's opinion for a crucial shot, surely you will trust his input. God's responses to your prayers may not come as quickly as you would like on the golf course, but I am confident He knows your situation and the desires of your heart.

By definition confidence is trust, assurance, boldness, and intimacy...even something confided in secret. We seem very comfortable when we are in the hands of a competent caddie or local professional. When your local tour professionals urge you on in a new grip or swing, you should have confidence that they are doing what they feel is best for you. If you don't feel that way, maybe you need to switch to another professional for help. Our Father in Heaven intends that we should have the ultimate confidence in him. It is what He is all about. He is all knowing, thus there is no need or reason to doubt that what He wants for you is best.

The quote above from Psalm 118:8 is the center verse in my Bible, and the two words "the Lord" are the two words at the very center. I cannot say what lies at the center of your Bible, but I can assure you that whatever those words are, they can be trusted. They will give you assurance, boldness, and confidence. It is a long-used, but not worn quote that says, "All scripture is given by inspiration of God, and is profitable for doctrine, reproof, for correction, for instruction in righteousness," (2 Timothy 3:16, KJV). A lack of confidence breeds doubt, and doubt can breed destruction. When you are standing over that critical shot, you have to concentrate to keep doubt from creeping in. You must focus on the task at hand, confident in your abilities, steady in your effort.

Just as "the Lord" is the center of my Bible, I have found that He must be the center of my life. Everything I do must glorify Him. I pray that when I meet Him in the sky, I will know Him with the confidence that will be eternal. I am, however, confident and trusting in what I know of His walk on this earth. I have the assurance that He is who he said he was; that His intimacy with me, through the person of the Holy Spirit, is who I should listen to with my heart. He arose and gave us the confidence of His life's work.

Your challenge today is to step out and gird up your confidence in your daily walk with the true master. You cannot imagine the changes that will be made in your life as you walk with Him. Ask Him to walk with you today as you make your way around the course. His companionship is beyond your expectations. He does not disappoint.

There Is One God

JWM

There is one God,
Creator,
And
Sustainer of all things,
Existing eternally,
In perfect Love
As
Father, Son and Holy Spirit.

I believe!

Warriors Of The Faith

"I exhort therefore, that first of all, supplications, prayers, intercessions, and giving of thanks, be made for all men; For kings, and for all that are in authority; that we may lead a quiet and peaceable life in all godliness and honesty. For this is good and acceptable in the sight of God our Savior; who will have all men to be saved and come unto the knowledge of the truth. For there is one God, and one mediator between God and men, the man Christ Jesus; who gave Himself a ransom for all, to be testified in due time," (1 Timothy 2: 1 - 6 KJV).

Thomas Jefferson was an American founding father who was the principal author of the Declaration of Independence and later served as the third President of the United States of America from 1801 to 1809. Previously he had served as the second Vice President of the United States under John Adams from 1797 to 1801. He died July 4. He once said, "I tremble for my country when I remember God is 'just.'"

Leading a quiet and peaceable life seems to be getting harder to do these days; with what appears in our daily news of discord and violence in our own land and the ever-present wars being fought overseas by our brave military. Guarding the rights and privileges, we so desperately cling to, are the responsibility of not only our government but one of the people. If we are to protect and defend our way of life and continue to embrace the history from which we draw our values, we must put our hearts and hands out to our Heavenly Father. He blessed our country, and those who fought both governments and foreign ideologies.

Supplications, prayers, intercessions, and giving of thanks are exhortations to be made by all men–for all men. We are not to discriminate between individuals, skip a few and shower others with our prayers and exhortations. After all, God gave his only son as a ransom for *all* of us…not a few of us. Our relatives, brave brothers and sisters, and fathers and mothers have given their lives over many eons of time to stand between the tyrannies that can overtake our peaceable way of life.

Defending one person is not unlike defending one nation. If one person stands for what is right, a nation can be born from the rattle that becomes a roil. So, it was with the United States of America. God placed in the hearts of brave men and women the desire to be free.

They came from places which had denied them the freedom they sought for themselves. Their plot was not only to arrive in the "free world" but to survive that world with all of its unknowns, dangers, and foreboding. They trusted our Father in heaven to protect them, guide them, and put before them a path to freedom. They gave their lives in sickness, dangerous seas, and death from Native Americans who rightly felt their land was being taken from them.

Being an American became the by-word for being a warrior for freedom and peacemaker among all men.

"These things I have spoken unto you, that in me ye might have peace. In the world ye shall have tribulation: but be of good cheer; I have overcome the world," (John 16:33, KJV).

We too should tremble at the knowledge that we serve a just God. He is the only true and fair judge, and His determination of what we have accomplished for Him, in His name and for the furtherance of His kingdom, will weigh heavy on judgement day. As our forefathers did in times before our birth, we must do for those yet to come, blazing a trail of truth and peace through the turbulence of this life to establish a solid ground for those who follow.

"Jesus didn't leave a material inheritance to his disciples. All He had when he died was a robe. But Jesus willed his followers something more valuable than gold. He willed us his peace. He said, 'My peace I give to you; not as the world gives'," (John 14:27, NKJV–Rev. Billy Graham)

A Psalm

AUTHOR UNKNOWN

The Lord is my Shepherd ---- that's a Relationship!
I shall not want ---- that's Supply!
He maketh me to lie down in green pastures ---- that's Rest!
He leadeth me beside the still waters ---- that's Refreshment!
He restoreth my soul ---- that's Healing!
He leadeth me in the paths of righteousness ---- that's Guidance!
For His name sake ---- that's Purpose!
Yea, though I walk through the valley of the shadow of death ---- that's Testing!
I will fear no evil ---- that's Protection!
For Thou art with me ---- that's Faithfulness!
Thy rod and Thy staff comfort me ---- that's Discipline!
Thou preparest a table before me in the presence of mine enemies ---- that's Hope!
Thou annointest my head with oil ---- that's Consecration!
My cup runneth over ---- that's Abundance!
Surely goodness and mercy shall follow me all the days of my life ---- that's Blessing!
And I will dwell in the house of the Lord ---- that's Security!
Forever ---- that's Eternity!

Balance

"Being confident of this very thing, that He which hath begun a good work in you will perform it until the day of Jesus Christ," (Philippians 1:6, KJV)

Those who are out of *balance* may conclude they do not need to do anything else–God will do whatever is needed. Once we have come to know our Lord, do we then relax and say to ourselves, "Well, that's it, I have done all I need to do, the rest is up to Him?" Do we really think that is all God is asking of us?

Of course not! We are asked to repent, sin not, love our neighbors, have charity, and share the Word to the ends of the earth. His love through us, after all, is our proof we belong to God. How can we do all of that if we are out of balance in our lives?

Striking a balance in our lives applies to so many areas of our person–who we are in total. You cannot drive a ball with any degree of consistency if you are constantly off balance. Neither can you putt well if you are not steady in your stance, balanced on your feet with your head down over the ball.

Lee Trevino said, "There are two things you can do with your head down, play golf and pray." Many of us have tried to do both at the same time.

Balancing a life in Christ and a life in this world is difficult for sure, yet we have the upper hand in that challenge. The flesh, the world, and even our pride can take our eyes off of Christ. These things are false prophets... offering us much, but yielding us nothing but heartache, disappointment, and trouble. We on the other hand have the love of God, the assurance of His only Son's gift of himself to us and the confidence in his return.

It is through His love for us that we can discern what is right and what is wrong. What His love instills in us provides the ability to properly weigh the challenges of our day to day lives. We then can use good judgement that brings balance to our lives.

"The odds of hitting a duffed shot increase by the square of the number of people watching," (Henry Beard, *Mulligan's Laws*).

People are watching. They have their eyes on you for sure, just wanting to see if you are real in your walk with the Lord. Can you balance your life in Christ with your personal walk? Does your life's game reflect your love for the Son? Take a moment today and determine if you are balanced. Are you leaning one way more than the other? Do you need to adjust your stance? Is your life on a level scale? You may want to take Lee Trevino's advice and put your head down... not to putt, but to pray.

We are Given All Things

ROMANS 8:32 KJV

"He that spared not His own Son, but delivered Him up for us all, how shall He not with Him also freely give us all things?"

Worthiness

"I, therefore, the prisoner of the Lord, beseech you that you walk worthy of the vocation wherewith ye are called, with all lowliness and meekness, with longsuffering, forbearing one another in love; endeavoring to keep the unity of the spirit in the bond of peace," (Ephesians 4:1, KJV).

Few of us were called to be professional golfers. In fact, a tiny percentage of those who get out on the course and try to emulate what they see on television actually have a game that could compete with the professional. Why is that?

It is not our vocation...we were not called to be a pro-golfer. At best, it is our avocation; it is what we do for our hobby to get-away with our golfing friends. That certainly does not make it any less challenging for the amateur player. Some may even wonder, "Why was I not more gifted in this game," "I work hard at the game; I know I am better than my scores reflect," or, "Am I not worthy of a better game?"

Yes, you as an individual are worthy, especially as you trust the Lord for your success. A laborer is worthy of his reward and you have no doubt put a lot of time and effort into your game. Then there is the nagging thought that squeaks out of the corner of the conversation with yourself, "Is this my reward, a 12 handicap?"

What you are encountering are distorted values. Practice doesn't make perfect... nothing does. You could practice morning, noon, and night and never reach perfection. Watch the pros. They have good days and bad.

"It is the one great democratic quirk of golf. Even the greatest players must occasionally stand by helplessly as their game disintegrates," (Michael Konik).

Your worth is illuminated in what you are called to do. You have sufficient value to do whatever the Lord has called you to perform. If you feel you have inadequate abilities or worth to take on a particular challenge, ask for His intercession. Call upon the Lord for increased strength to accomplish what you have set out to do. Don't let the attempt for perfection get you down. Strive to be better. All of the disciples struggled with their worthiness. That feeling of not being worthy to serve Him had to be in each of their hearts in the beginning. What He did for them, He will do for you. He will build you up so that you can perform the tasks He puts before you. You will have the strength to stand up for your belief in Him, to share His message and to be worthy of the vocation wherewith you were called.

Throughout Biblical history, there have been those who felt they were unworthy to serve our great God. Considering his own past, Moses must have questioned Saul regarding his own debacles, "How can I be worthy to serve?"

When you realize your calling was not to be the best golfer in the world, then ask yourself, "Just what is it that the Lord *has* called me to do?" Better yet, go to Him on your knees and seek His response to your question. He will answer, He is no doubt preparing you, He will strengthen you and show you your *worth* is based in His love for you. You will then find that you are indeed a prisoner of the Lord and worthy of His love.

Moment in Prayer

JWM

A moment in prayer,
Is like an hour in the Lord's ear.

Contentment

"Not that I speak in respect of want: for I have learned, in whatsoever state I am, therewith to be content. I know both how to be abased, and I know how to abound: everywhere and in all things, I am instructed both to be full and to be hungry, both to abound and to suffer need. I can do all things through Christ which strengtheneth me," (Philippians 4: 11-13, KJV).

While in a Roman prison, Paul wrote, "[I have] learned in whatsoever state I am, therewith to be content." Thinking about that statement, one can reach a very important destination as far as your daily state of mind is concerned. It is not continuous euphoria or even that of being exceedingly happy every day. No, it is a point of confidence in knowing that our Father in heaven holds us lovingly in his hands always. He will never leave us or forsake us.

As we grow from childhood to adulthood, we also begin desiring more–more of almost everything. We are insatiable in some things, never being able to have all of, or nearly all of whatever strikes our fancy at any given point in life. When we do receive what fills our long-held desires, then we quickly move on to something else. It may not be the next most desirable, but we tend to slide up the scale a bit in our wants and quickly forget the last most important thing, moving on to the next important thing. We experience that dreaded disappointment when our desires are not met. But should we?

As this is written the world is in the throes of the COVID-19 pandemic. There is a tremendous amount of uncertainty in the air, from one corner of the globe to the other. Yet even with the uncertainties, there is calm in the minds and hearts of those who are given over to our Lord Jesus Christ; as those who know Him are secure in his safe keeping. In verse 13 of the above quote Paul states, "I can do all things through Christ which strengtheneth me." Those placing themselves in His hands are content, satisfied if you will, that He, being ultimately in charge of all things, will see us through this pandemic and will restore a healthy order to his creation.

Sitting in our easy chairs and accepting that He will take care of things for us is not the total contentment I believe is intended for us. Taking part in our contentment is also taking part in the design God has for us in being able to fulfill our wants and needs. There is activity required in being content. One cannot just stand by and expect peace; it has to be worked for. One cannot stand by and expect success; it too has to be worked for. Yet contentment can be enjoyed through the work. Satisfaction is gained when production has accomplished its goal. Work has revealed its reward. There is nothing quite like leaving a job, whatever it might be, knowing you have done all your talents would allow in reaching a certain level of success. There is a natural sigh that follows.

We cannot be protected from everything that is thrown at us, but we can stand firm in our belief that Christ is with us through it all. That one fact will provide the contentment that no other belief can approach.

Contentment–the ability to abound in the love of Christ in whatever situation we find ourselves–be it even in prison for our true faith in our Lord Jesus Christ.

Because of Jesus

REV. BILLY GRAHAM

"Because of what Jesus Christ did for us
Through His cross and resurrection,
We know that we have hope for the future."

Forgiveness

"Then said Jesus, Father, forgive them; for they know not what they do," (Luke 23:34 KJV).

Take a moment and repeat that quote in your mind. Yes, it was actually spoken by our Lord, under circumstances beyond our imagining, far from our being able to understand the depth of its meaning. Can we even grasp what He was asking the Father to do?

Forgiveness is essential in life. I am not talking about the *forgiving* holes on a golf course, the ones you know you can use to make up strokes. Nor am I talking about the slip of the tongue or exasperations you sometimes let go under your breath. They need to be acknowledged by you with repentance and forgiven by those offended. These offenses become a scar when they are not entirely forgiven and put aside.

The forgiveness we need to focus on is our Lord's forgiveness of the sin that sent Him to the cross for us. It wasn't just the sin of the people of the day in Christ's time. It was all the sin, then and now, which we have committed...all of us.

Forgiveness can be such a difficult thing to understand. Not forgiving someone for an offense, whether intended or otherwise, can ruin a wonderful relationship, especially if that person is close to you, such as your spouse, your child, a parent, or even a playing partner. On the other hand, forgiving someone for an offense can lift you up in a way you cannot imagine. It will also remove the burden of the offense from the person who committed it. Forgiving someone will clear your heart of a malady for which there is no other medicine.

Our Lord had been delivered to Calvary after being shamed, beaten, and ultimately exchanged for a murderer. Crowds who had listened to His words prior, called for Him to be crucified. So now we arrive when the words came from His lips, "Father, forgive them; for they know not what they do." Beyond our earthly understanding, these words ring down through the centuries to our generation. He has forgiven those who have sinned against Him and those who were to sin against Him in the time to come. He asks, through His inerrant word, that you open the door, "Behold, I stand at the door, and knock: if any man hear my voice, and open the door, I will come in to him, and will sup with him, and he with Me," (Revelation 3:20 KJV).

Removing the burden of needing to forgive someone, and even forgiving yourself, will not only energize your life and those who are forgiven, but will calm your heart. Your nerves will settle. Your mind will clear the fog of stagnation which resulted from your constantly revisiting the offense. Once forgiveness moves in, there is no room for bitterness or spite. Your hand will be the first to reach out to a once embittered relationship.

There will be no yips when forgiving, no hooks or slices, no duffed shots...forgiveness settles the score, acknowledges the handicaps and allows life's course to be played with a partner who is in true harmony with you. Having repented, your Father in Heaven will forgive you and will call on you to forgive as He has done.

"In one bold stroke, forgiveness obliterates the past and permits us to enter the land of new beginnings," (Rev. Billy Graham).

He Chose You

"For ye see your calling, brethren, how that not many wise men after the flesh, not many mighty, not many noble, are called," (1 Cor. 1:26, KJV).

In God's wisdom, the teacher is also our Savior. When we come to Him in faith, "Of Him are ye in Christ Jesus, who of God is made unto us wisdom, and righteousness, and sanctification, and redemption. That, according as it is written, He that glorieth, let him glory in the Lord," (1 Cor. 1:30-31, KJV).

"The Bible is filled with stories of how God used weak, unlikely, or flawed characters to bring about His purposes. Included in that lineup are Abraham, Isaac, Jacob, Moses, Rahab, Gideon and Peter–just to name a few. God chose elderly Abraham and his barren wife to be 'The father (and mother) of many nations,' (Genesis 17:5). He used Isaac, who played favorites (25:27-28), and Jacob, a deceiver, to continue that line (25:29-34; 27:1-29). God called the reluctant Moses, a murderer on the run, to lead His people out of slavery in Egypt (Exodus 2:11-15; 14:1-31). God chose the prostitute Rahab to hide the spies in Jericho (Joshua 2) and to be included in the genealogy of Jesus (Matthew 1:5); he called Gideon, who cowered in fear, to serve as judge and rescue the Israelites from the Midianites (Judges 6-8); and He appointed Peter, an outspoken fisherman, to be His disciple (Matthew 16:22). God still uses flawed characters – you and me- to fulfill His purposes." (Taken from Our Daily Bread, July 17, 2018)

READ: (especially verse 16)

Matthew 5:1-16

The Beatitudes

Every man and woman, who follows Christ, must stand for something that furthers His Kingdom. Now, today, you are that person!

Dactylogram Of Christ

What is it about man that so strongly reflects the design of the Creator?

Is it our physical makeup? The nuts and bolts, blood and bones and the sinew that holds us together are in each and every one of us, establishing the truth that we are made equal under God's hand. Christ came into this world and bore a fate so astonishing it stunned the world. Not only in His time but in our time and eternity to come, He has imprinted upon each of us the fingerprint of the divine, Jesus Christ our Lord.

In Christ Jesus, we find the immutable living proof that the Word is indeed the sword of the Spirit. Thus it is the source of all strength, allowing each of us to stand and act boldly in perseverance, proclaiming the gospel.

"Wherefore take unto you the whole armour of God, that you may be able to withstand in the evil day, and having done all, to stand. Stand therefore, having your loins girt about with truth, and having on the breastplate of righteousness; and your feet shod with the preparation of the Gospel of peace; above all, taking the shield of faith, wherewith ye shall be able to quench all the fiery darts of the wicked. And take the helmet of salvation, and the sword of the spirit, which is the Word of God: praying always with all prayer and supplication in the Spirit, and watching thereunto with all perseverance and supplication for all saints; and for me, that utterance may be given unto me, that I may open my mouth boldly, to make known the mystery of the Gospel, for which I am ambassador in bonds: that therein I may speak boldly, as I ought to speak," (Ephesians 6:13-20, KJV).

The embodiment of strength lies within Christ Jesus our Lord and Savior. He possesses the totality of all strength and thus, in all situations, stands firm and right. He was always bold in his statements and in his storytelling. By way of parables, he stated what was right without equivocation. Always on point, His parables were given to provoke thought and direction which indicated to the hearer the righteous path one should follow. During his time on earth, He remained humble, but not weak, fiercely strong, yet compassionate.

"The Lord reigneth, He is clothed with majesty; the Lord is clothed with strength, wherewith he hath girded himself: the world also is established that it cannot be moved," (Psalm 93:1, KJV).

"God is our refuge and strength, a very present help in trouble," (Psalm 46:1, KJV).

"Trust ye in the Lord forever: for in the Lord JEHOVAH is everlasting strength," (Isaiah 26:4, KJV).

It is clear there is no other power in this universe which is beyond that of our God. Within the Trinity of God, the Father, God the Son, and God the Holy Spirit, lay the origin and backbone to our own strengths. The source of your human strength originates at birth and was predestined by the Father of all strength. We can choose to develop what we have been given or we can ignore what one might call our natural abilities and thus waste the gift.

The point can be drawn succinctly in the above quote from Isaiah 26:4 in that the strength we have is given up at death and we then are to be embraced by the power of God as we praise Him as the Lord JEHOVAH, the eternal source of all everlasting strength.

This gift of strength is but one of the fingerprints of Christ, so gifted to each of us as to be the bedrock for all other gifts. It is as if He had stated to each of us personally, "Upon this rock I will build my church." We are to use the strength He gave us, in all its applications, to build His kingdom, and to further the Gospel.

Peace

NUMBERS 6:24-26 KJV

"The Lord bless thee, and keep thee:
the Lord make His face to shine upon thee,
and be gracious unto thee:
the Lord lift up His countenance upon thee:
and give thee peace."

Liberty

"Where the Spirit of the Lord is, there is Liberty," (2 Corinthians 3:17 KJV).

Father's Day is annually celebrated across the land and with much fanfare. I am sure Fathers were smothered in hugs, kisses, and treated to their most favorite foods. Some fired up the bar-b-que, some watched the US Open Golf Tournament, some even got out on the course and played a round… or even two.

Since being separated by many, many miles from my grown children, my hugs and kisses were of the long-distance cell-phone type. They were appreciated none the less, and it was heartwarming to hear their voices and the nice things they had to say. My favorite dish was enjoyed while we dined out with good friends.

It was a memorable day. We had the freedom to go where we wanted, eat what we wanted, with the folks with whom we wanted to share our day. In fact, we had the *liberty* to do whatever we pleased.

Liberty is a concept that has come down through the ages. Without changing much in definition, it means a release from bondage, imprisonment, or control of another. It even means an exemption from slavery. Ah! This is one with which we can all identify. We know what slavery was, and many of us have a more recent memory of a kind of slavery that is closer to us than that for which the Civil War was fought. It is the concept of controlling another or being under another's control. Work, business meetings, and your outside responsibilities can begin to overwhelm you. Those outside forces can become a master to you...unless you can reach into that reservoir of liberty that is Jesus Christ.

Before we accepted Christ as our Savior, we were all captives of sin. We can be held back as if we are slaves to our own desires. We were wanting, but not sure what we wanted or needed. What we find in accepting Christ is that there is liberty in our walk, a liberty that is unknown before coming to Him. There is newness now, a reassurance of right, a purpose to our walk. Your friends and family see it. Your fellow workers and even your golfing partners see it. This is the liberty that ensures that you are not a stumbling block to others, but rather a helping hand. Not an advantage taker, but an advantage giver.

In our church service on Father's Day, our youth pastor spoke. His words were not unlike other pastors who spoke on Sunday around the country, but it was poignant. Included in the context of Fathers were the Christian men who have been mentors, guides, kindred hearts, and father figures. Those are men who have and are experiencing liberty in Christ. These men are flesh and blood and stand before us as role models. Let us not forget that our Lord is our supreme role model, and it is through imitating Him that we will be able to stand tall in the eyes of those who look to us to point the way. We should hold to the liberty He offers, until the day He returns, and liberates us into His presence.

Moral Leadership

REV. BILLY GRAHAM

"Truly, the world is in need of moral leadership...
that teaches the difference between right and wrong
and teaches us to forgive one another even as we are forgiven
by our Father in heaven."

The Tee, The Cross And Resurrection

The three most important events in history are the virgin birth, death, and resurrection of our Lord Jesus Christ. Not everyone will agree with that statement, but it is the place from which I will begin.

To many, the cross was not the end…nor was it a new beginning; it was a promise of continuance and a confirmation of the words Jesus had spoken. Remember? In John 11:25 KJV he stated, "I am the resurrection and the life." He was telling us that through His resurrection we would find life as we had never known it before. Without His resurrection, life would be meaningless. Without His resurrection, the cross would be meaningless. His life and His teachings go on, surviving the centuries and continuing to provide grace, mercy, love, and compassion.

When Martha approached Him, in John 11:40 KJV, Jesus stated, "Said I not unto thee, that if thou wouldest believe, thou shouldest see the glory of God?" We should take solid footing in His words and believe as Martha did when she witnessed the resurrection of her brother Lazarus. The scriptures said Christ would rise in three days, and He did. If you are a believer, you take those words literally. Others may doubt still, but the proof is in what He has done since His resurrection. To millions of those who have believed on Him and had their lives changed, He is the living Son of God. The fruit of His life here on earth continues to confirm His divinity.

I cannot resurrect my golf game. It has been too long in the locker of time. Many years have gone by since I last held a club in my hand and planted my tee in the ground with the confidence, I was going to finally have the drive of a lifetime. Too many times that feeling was rewarded with reality - another bad drive. I failed many times in front of my friends, fellow players, peers, and even family members. What keeps us coming back? What speaks to that private space in our minds, "I know I can do this; I just need to keep believing I can"?

In my opinion, it is not that we cannot do something like hitting a golf ball straight for two hundred plus yards. It is that we consistently resurrect the old stuff, the bad stuff. Habits that we have not changed in order to make progress in our game have risen to inflict that ever-crushing feeling...doubt! It takes work to make progress. It takes study to make any advance in our life's game. Our golf game may suffer from our lack of talent or ability, but our walk with Christ will never suffer from our lack of talent or ability. After all, He made us, breathed life into us, and was resurrected in order to act as our intercessor and shepherd to bring us into an eternal life with Him.

Let each of us believe in Christ's love and see the glory of God. The resurrection was, and remains, the stake in the ground that signifies not an ending, not a new beginning, but the confirmation of the continuance of Christ's promises. Believing on Him *will* allow us to see the glory of God.

As you put that little wooden tee in the ground on the first hole, remember the cross, how He got there, how He died there, how He arose to offer you eternal life through Himself. He overcame death and the world...for you.

He is no Fool

PHILIP JAMES ELLIOT, 1927-1956

"He is no fool who gives what he cannot keep to gain what he cannot lose."

Traditions

The Apostle Paul wrote in 2 Thessalonians 2:15-17, "Therefore, brethren, stand fast, and hold the traditions which ye have been taught, whether by word, or our epistle. Now our Lord Jesus Christ himself, and God, even our Father, which hath loved us, and hath given us everlasting consolation and good hope through grace, comfort your hearts and establish you in every good word and work," (KJV).

The passing of time, which births the generations, yields the traditions which flow endlessly, as do the tides of time continue to wash its treasures upon the shores. Incorporating the values, both of family and community, the newborn child learns from those who care for it. It learns the knowledge it will need to persevere, the wisdom to rightly decide, and the love to share that others may gain from those things valued by the individual.

Those of us who have reached our "three score and ten" and now gone beyond, have a responsibility to those who will follow. We are responsible to leave behind the pearls of our wisdom we have gained through the knowledge and personal relationship with our Savior Jesus Christ. We may call them whatever we like, but most tend to call them traditions. So, they may be until you have come to a personal knowledge of Christ. Those so-called traditions are not the Thanksgiving, or Christmas holiday trappings we tend to associate with the seasons. The traditions we leave in the pursuit of knowing Christ leave a bigger footprint than those only at holiday seasons.

The older generations must leave behind the standard, the responsibility to be carried on of spreading the word, witnessing to not only our own family members but to the members of the world community at large. It is a small meal that drops from the mouth of a wren, but a banquet that falls to the side of the anthill. What we know as individuals may seem small to us, but it can be a pearl of untapped knowledge to someone who has not heard the Word. If all we have are the seasonal traditions in our life, we are missing greatly the spirit of our truest responsibility, that of following and spreading the word of our Lord and Savior.

If we truly want to have traditions and follow them throughout the year, then let them be of a greater purpose than those for just the holidays. Let them be those which are not apart from the word of God. Let them be brought under the Word, as we are truly transparent beings if our words and actions do not mirror our Lord and creator. Paul states in Galatians 4:3, "Even so we, when we were children, were in bondage under the elements of the world," (KJV). Are we not to leave behind a compass so that others can find their way? Since as little children we are "in bondage under the elements of the world," do we not feel a heavy responsibility to define what a Christian tradition should reflect?

Apart from the word of God, we are nothing. Our knowledge culminates into the wisdom we will pass along. Our Christian traditions must reflect the light that we have received through the knowledge of His word.

"And the things that thou hast heard of me among many witnesses, the same commit thou to faithful men, who shall be able to teach others also," (2 Timothy 2:2, KJV).

A Prayer in Rebirth

JWM

Father, I am but a common man,
And come to you upon my knees;
To ask forgiveness in my rebirth,
To share my life and needs.

The peace I seek is yours to give,
For all who seek will find;
Let Thy grace enter in,
And grant me peace of mind.

As I enter in upon your light,
And ask Thy prayer for me;
Lend Thy comfort to my soul,
And guide me through eternity.

Rest my anguished heart from wrong,
And shine Thy light on me;
Place my heart on the righteous path,
Jesus prepared for me.

About The Author

John W. McCall is just a southern boy from Charlotte, North Carolina who entered the United States Air Force at the age of 19 and retired from it in 1986. He always wanted to live by the sea and made a promise to Marla, his wife of 26 years, and himself that he would be there by the time he was 70. Being a Carolina brat, he always figured that would put him somewhere around Myrtle Beach, South Carolina. John and Marla moved to within walking distance of the beach...in Southern Oregon, having moved there one month before his 70th birthday. The McCalls now live in Washington near the beautiful Hood Canal.

www.ingramcontent.com/pod-product-compliance
Lightning Source LLC
Chambersburg PA
CBHW071856160426
43209CB00005B/1082